LITTLE MOON
Blue Whale

ABE
Abyssinian Jackal

STELLA
Steller's Sea Cow

TRICK
Javan Tiger

ELLIOT
California Condor

Meet the inhabitants of No Man's Valley, a magical place
where endangered—and even extinct—animals live in
peace and harmony. Here they are safe from humans
and the problems of the outside world. In this book
you will encounter some of the most colorful citizens of
this enchanted land.

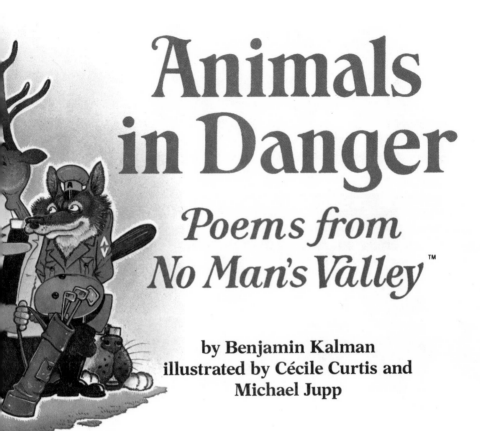

Animals in Danger

Poems from No Man's Valley ™

by Benjamin Kalman
illustrated by Cécile Curtis and
Michael Jupp

Random House/New York

Copyright © 1982 by Frank Fehmers Publishing b.v. No Man's Valley is a trademark of Frank Fehmers Publishing b.v. Based upon an idea by Harrie Geelen. All rights reserved under International and Pan-American Copyright Conventions. Published in the United States by Random House, Inc., New York, and simultaneously in Canada by Random House of Canada Limited, Toronto. *Library of Congress Cataloging in Publication Data:* Kalman, Benjamin. Animals in danger. SUMMARY: A collection of poems about a valley where such endangered and extinct animals as the dodo, panda, and blue whale live together in peace and harmony. 1. Rare animals—Juvenile poetry. 2. Extinct animals—Juvenile poetry. 3. Wildlife conservation—Juvenile poetry. 4. Children's poetry, American. [1. Rare animals—Poetry. 2. Extinct animals—Poetry. 3. Wildlife conservation—Poetry. 4. American poetry] I. Curtis, Cécile, ill. II. Jupp, Michael, ill. III. Title. PS3561.A41666A5 811'.54 82-3827 AACR2 ISBN: 0-394-85454-3 (trade); 0-394-95454-8 (lib. bdg.) Manufactured in the United States of America 1 2 3 4 5 6 7 8 9 0

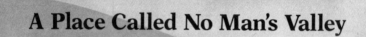

A Place Called No Man's Valley

There's a place called No Man's Valley
Where no man is ever seen,
Where the water's bright and sparkling
And the grass is fresh and green.
There the animals are happy,
Free to hop or flop or run,
For they know that in that valley
There will never be a gun.

Many species are endangered
And their numbers grow each day,
So they flock to No Man's Valley
Where they all may safely stay.
It is pleasant, it is peaceful,
And the air is always clear
In that place called No Man's Valley
Where no creature lives in fear.

Dodo
(Raphus cucullatus)

Dodos once abounded on the island of Mauritius in the Indian Ocean. They were large, flightless birds with few natural defenses and, fortunately, no natural enemies. European explorers began to arrive on Mauritius in the early 1600s along with their domestic pigs and dogs. These animals preyed on the dodo population, and sailors from visiting ships fed on the dodo. By the end of the seventeenth century the dodos had been exterminated.

Oh Dodo, Dear Dodo

Oh dodo, dear dodo,
Poor doddering bird,
Your body was dumpy,
Your face was absurd,
Your walk was a waddle,
You never could fly,
Your wings were not meant
For a trip to the sky.

Oh dodo, dear dodo,
Ungainly and round,
You never quite managed
To get off the ground.
You never were clever,
You always were shy,
You're no more, poor dodo,
And never knew why.

Giant Panda
(Ailuropoda melanoleuca)

Although the giant panda looks like a bear, it is a unique species. It is found only in the high altitudes of the Hsifan mountains near the former Tibetan border in China. The giant panda has been under the full protection of the Chinese government since 1939 and is considered a national treasure. There are about four thousand giant pandas alive today.

The Panda

The panda is a quiet sort
With little else to do
Than sit and chew on tasty shoots
Of succulent bamboo.

Its nose is pug, its ears are round,
It's like a cuddly bear,
A patchy coat of black and white
Is what it likes to wear.

The panda asks for nothing
But maintains a happy mood
As it roams about the mountains
In its peaceful solitude.

Blue Whale
(Balaenoptera musculus)

Blue whales are the largest animals that have ever lived on earth. They can grow to a length of 108 feet. They are now completely protected and very rare. Whalers always hunted the blue whale because it is the largest, and therefore the most profitable, whale to catch. Blue whales migrate to the polar regions in spring and back to warmer regions in fall. They can live for thirty years.

The Whopping Blue Whale

The whopping blue whale is a whale of a whale,
She's a whale of an undersea mountain,
She's built on a thundering whale of a scale
And she spouts a spectacular fountain.

The whopping blue whale has a whale of a tail
That occasions a whale of commotion,
For she leaves a gargantuan whale of a trail
As she flips and she flails through the ocean.

Compared to the whale, even elephants pale,
And children seem smaller than fleas,
But unless we stop hunting the whopping blue whale,
The giants will be gone from the seas.

Quagga
(Equus quagga)

The quagga was related to and resembled the zebra;
the front of its body was striped, the rear was not.
When European settlers moved into Africa, they used
the quagga as a work animal and often slaughtered it
to provide meat for the farm workers. By the early
twentieth century the quagga was virtually extinct.

The Quagga

The quagga, in a quandary,
Was disgruntled and distressed,
For it could not quite determine
How it wanted to be dressed.

It wore zebra-striped pajamas
From its middle to its nose,
But the bottom of the quagga
Was attired in donkey's clothes.

It's no longer in a quandary,
Its extinction is complete,
For that indecisive quagga
Was delectable to eat.

Garlic Toad, or European Spadefoot Toad
(Pelobates fuscus)

The garlic toad was formerly found in sandy lowlands throughout western Europe. It is now protected in Italy and the Netherlands. It has a sharp-edged "shovel" on the inside of each foot, ideal for burrowing in the soft sand. As garlic toads are rarely seen aboveground during the day, little is known about them. Their popular name is derived from the unpleasant odor they emit when frightened.

Garlic Toads

Garlic toads feel safe and happy
As they hop from stone to stone,
For a toad that smells like garlic
Is a toad that's left alone.

Garlic toads are unmolested,
They discourage all their foes,
Any enemy that nears them
Runs away and holds its nose.

Garlic toads are also homely,
All the same, I wish them well,
For I'd really sort of miss them...
Though I would not miss their smell.

California Condor
(Gymnogyps californianus)

The California condor has been on earth for more than seventy million years and once thrived throughout most of North America. This majestic bird—which has a nine-foot wingspread—now lives only in southern California, where urban development is rapidly destroying its natural environment. Two decades ago there were believed to be sixty condors left on earth; today there are no more than twenty-four.

The California Condor

The California condor
Is the largest bird that flies,
With its great majestic wingspread
It's the monarch of the skies.

The California condor
Rarely congregates in crowds,
It spends its time on mountaintops
And contemplates the clouds.

But if mankind keeps encroaching
On the mountains where they thrive,
Then the California condors
Are unlikely to survive.

Steller's Sea Cow
(Eumetopias jubata)

Steller's sea cow was discovered in 1741 on Bering Island by a stranded crew of explorers. It was named after the ship's doctor and naturalist, Georg Wilhelm Steller. Fur hunters slaughtered the peaceful animals for their meat and their inch-thick skin, which was used to make boats and shoes. Steller's sea cow became extinct only twenty-seven years after it was discovered. There have been recent sightings of what appears to be this creature, but scientists have not yet confirmed these reports.

Steller's Sea Cow

There was a clumsy mermaid
In a coat of wrinkled skin,
Her name was Steller's sea cow,
She had bristles on her chin.

Her ears were very tiny
And her body very big,
Her head was sometimes covered
With a sort of seaweed wig.

Steller's sea cow lives no longer,
She is lost to you and me,
The most unlikely mermaid
Ever seen beneath the sea.

Javan Tiger
(Panthera tigris sondaica)

Pollution, the destruction of their habitats, and the
greed of hunters who want to sell their spectacular
pelts for fur coats have made the Javan tiger the most
endangered of all tiger species. In spite of conservation
laws, there are thought to be less than a dozen left in
the dense forests of Javan game preserves.

Imagine if Tigers...

Imagine if tigers
Were simply no more,
No bright tiger beauty,
No loud tiger roar,
No tiger to run,
Putting creatures to flight,
No tiger-eye gleam
In the forest at night.

No glint of a fang
In a great tiger jaw,
No sheathing, unsheathing,
Of sharp tiger claw.
Though I don't want them here
In my own neighborhood,
How empty the world
If they vanished for good.

Square-Lipped or White Rhinoceros
(Ceratotherium simum)

The square-lipped or white rhinoceros—the largest species of rhinoceros—is much more docile and gentle than its cousin, the black rhinoceros. It was once hunted near to extinction because its horn was believed to contain substances beneficial to human beings. Today the white rhinoceros is protected by law in South Africa, but there are perhaps less than a thousand left of the northern race in East Africa.

The Enormous White Rhinoceros

The enormous white rhinoceros
Is practically unique,
With horns beneath his forehead
And a cumbersome physique.

He is bulky, he is bulgy,
Long and lumpy, high and wide,
He has wrinkles on the wrinkles
On the wrinkles of his hide.

His eyes are weak, his skull is thick,
His brain is rather dim,
And he will never bother you
If you don't bother him.

Abyssinian Jackal
(Canis simensis)

Jackals are closely related to wolves in appearance and habit. They feed almost exclusively on rodents and do not attack domestic cattle as some people believe. Though still endangered, there is hope for the species. A national park now being established in Ethiopia will protect three to four hundred of these beautiful animals.

The Abyssinian Jackal

The Abyssinian jackal
Has a big and bushy tail,
It is reddish brown in color,
Though its chin is rather pale.

Its snout is long and tapered,
And its cry is high and weird,
It was hunted through the centuries
Till it almost disappeared.

But its once uncertain future
Does not seem to be so black,
For the jackal's now protected...
So the jackal will be back.

Extinction Is Forever

Many creatures on our planet
Face the catastrophic fate
Of complete eradication;
For a few it is too late.

We must do our best to save them,
We must help them to survive,
For the world will be much richer
If they all remain alive.

Should we drive them to extinction
It would be a tragic crime,
For extinction is forever,
and forever means ALL TIME!

MAYOR PANDA
Giant Panda

QUANDARY
Quagga

LOUIS
Garlic Toad

DEADY
Dodo

WHITEY
White Rhinoceros